Table of Contents

1 2 3 4 5 / 10 09 08 07 06

D1555664

Know Your Map Skills
Geography Centers • Grades 1–2

Let's Get Started!

The ten learning centers in this book are self-contained units that target important skills and concepts in engaging formats. Prepare each center according to its instructions to create self-directed learning experiences for your students. Then place the pocket folder centers in a container in a convenient spot in the classroom where students can access them easily for independent work. Once the centers are assembled, use them anytime during the school year at the appropriate places in the curriculum. The need for student supervision is minimal as the centers are self-explanatory and self-correcting. Make sure students know where to place their work once it is complete.

Each of the ten full-color centers includes:

- **instructions for the teacher** that provide how-to information and a description of the activities
- **instructions for students** that explain how to use the various center elements
- **components** needed to construct and manage each center
- **reproducible** worksheets and other materials for student use
- **self-checking answer keys** for immediate feedback

   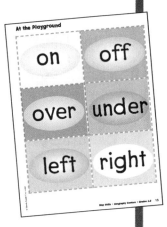

Using Centers in Your Classroom

There are several ways to integrate the learning centers in this book into the classroom routine. Each learning center is designed to reinforce previously introduced concepts. Familiarize students with each center by presenting the skill and center components to the large group. Draw attention to the student instruction sheet, which is designed to be placed on the back of each pocket folder. This page provides detailed information to ensure that students can work independently. Then invite students to work in pairs or alone to complete the activities.

The centers contain games and puzzles as well as paper-and-pencil activities to provide a rich and varied learning experience. Try augmenting the materials provided with your favorite independent learning tools to further enhance and reinforce skill development.

Page 4 is a center checklist to facilitate record-keeping. Place it in the area of the classroom designated for centers, allowing students to record their progress. Or use it as a personal record-keeping device to enter data about students' progress and accomplishments at each center.

Create a Center Using Pocket Folders

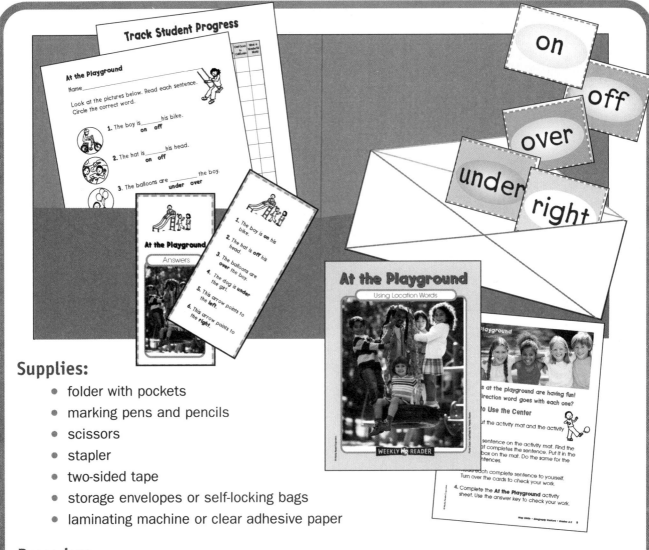

Supplies:

- folder with pockets
- marking pens and pencils
- scissors
- stapler
- two-sided tape
- storage envelopes or self-locking bags
- laminating machine or clear adhesive paper

Procedure:

1. Remove the folder cover page from the book. Photocopy any text that is on the back of this page. Then laminate the cover page. Affix it to the front of the folder.

2. Detach the student instructions page. Laminate and attach it to the back of the folder.

3. Remove the self-checking answer key for each center activity sheet. Laminate and cut the page in half to create a cover page and answer key. Staple the cover page on top of the answer key. Place the answer key in the left folder pocket.

4. Place center checklists, reproducibles, and other materials in the left folder pocket.

5. Laminate any activity cards or game pieces. Place each set of cards in a labeled envelope or self-locking bag. Place the labeled envelopes in the right folder pocket.

6. Store the folder centers in a box or file crate. Students can take folders to their desks or a table to complete the tasks.

Track Student Progress

Student Names	At the Playground	Match A Map	Hi, Neighbor!	Getting Directions	Which Way?	What Is a Map Key?	Land or Water?	U.S. Neighbors	Carl Goes to California	What a Wonderful World

☆ ☆ ☆ ☆ ☆ ☆ ☆ ☆ ☆ ☆ ☆ ☆ ☆ ☆ ☆ ☆ ☆ ☆ ☆

Hi, Neighbor!

Learning About a Neighborhood Map

Get Ready!

- Prepare a folder following directions on page 3. Student instructions are on page 33, an activity mat is on page 35, activity cards are on page 37, and the answer key is on page 39.

- Make copies of the reproducible activity sheet on page 30 and put them in the left folder pocket.

- Laminate and cut apart the activity cards. Place the activity cards in an envelope or a self-locking bag. Put the activity mat and activity cards in the right folder pocket.

- Invite students to take the activity mat and cards from the folder. Tell students to choose an activity card to place in the correct box on the mat. The back of the cards provide self-checking answers.

- Have students complete the reproducible activity sheet. Students can check their answers by using the answer key.

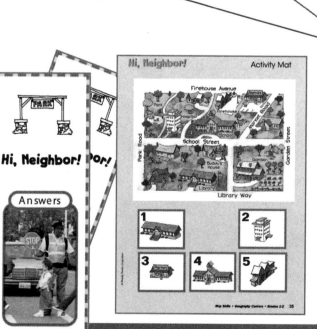

Hi, Neighbor!

Name_____

Read each sentence. Look at the picture map found on the activity mat. Circle the correct word or words.

1. A park is near the _____.   **hospital**   **library**

2. The market is near the _____.   **library**   **firehouse**

3. The school is on _____.
    Garden Street   **School Street**

4. A red house has a _____.   **park**   **garden**

5. The library is on _____.
    Firehouse Avenue   **Library Way**

6. The color of the school is _____.   **yellow**   **blue**

Hi, Neighbor!

Learning About a Neighborhood Map

WEEKLY **WR** READER

Hi, Neighbor!

This neighborhood map shows pictures
Of homes and streets and trees.
Each picture stands for a real thing
A thing you've probably seen.

How to Use the Center

1. Take out the activity mat and the activity cards. Look at the map.

2. Choose the card with a photograph of a real hospital on it. Place that card on top of the picture of a hospital. Do the same for the other cards.

3. Turn the cards over to check your work.

4. Complete the **Hi, Neighbor!** activity sheet.

5. Use the answer key to check your work.

N

W

E

S

Hi, Neighbor!

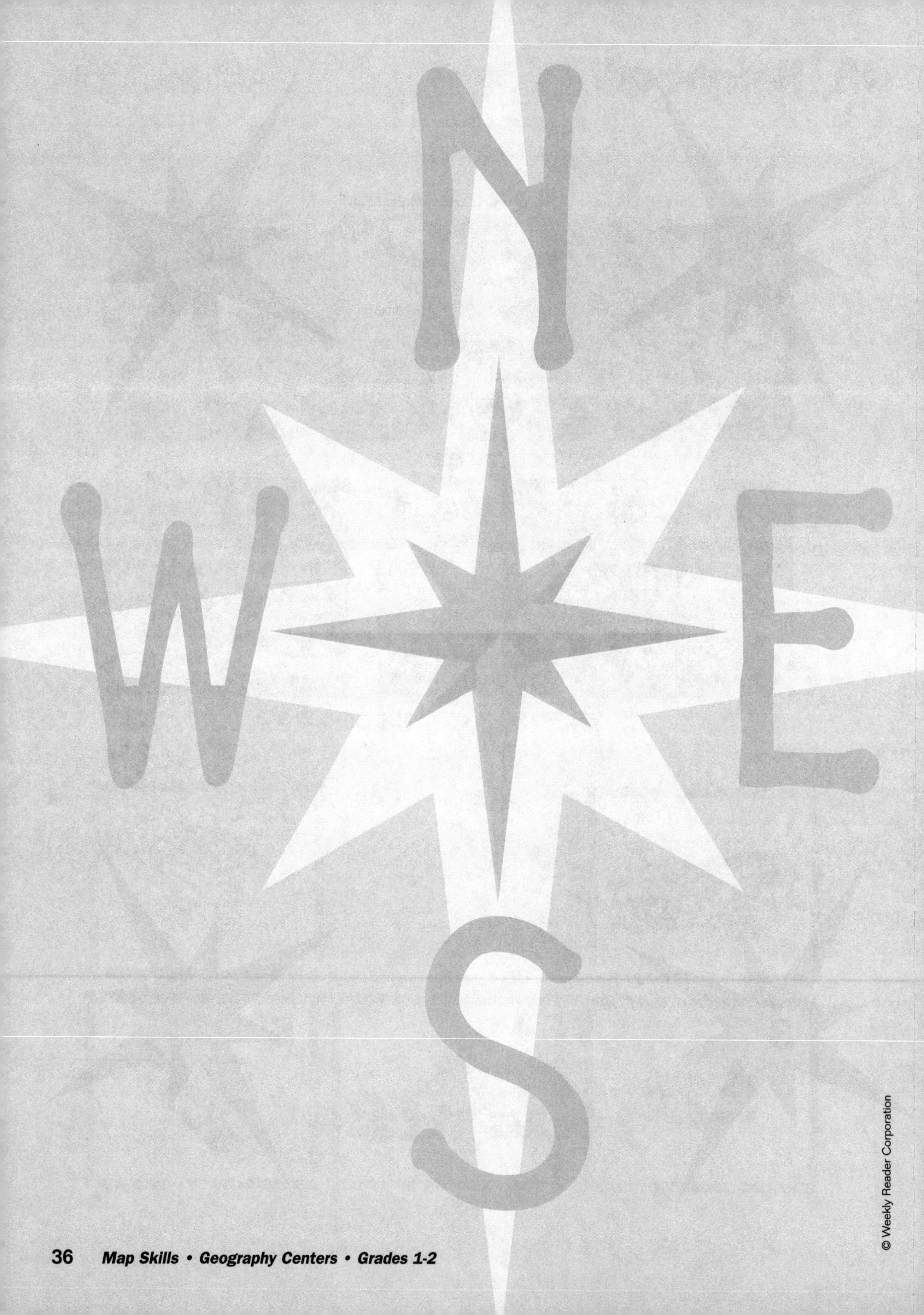
N
W
E
S

Hi, Neighbor!
Activity Cards

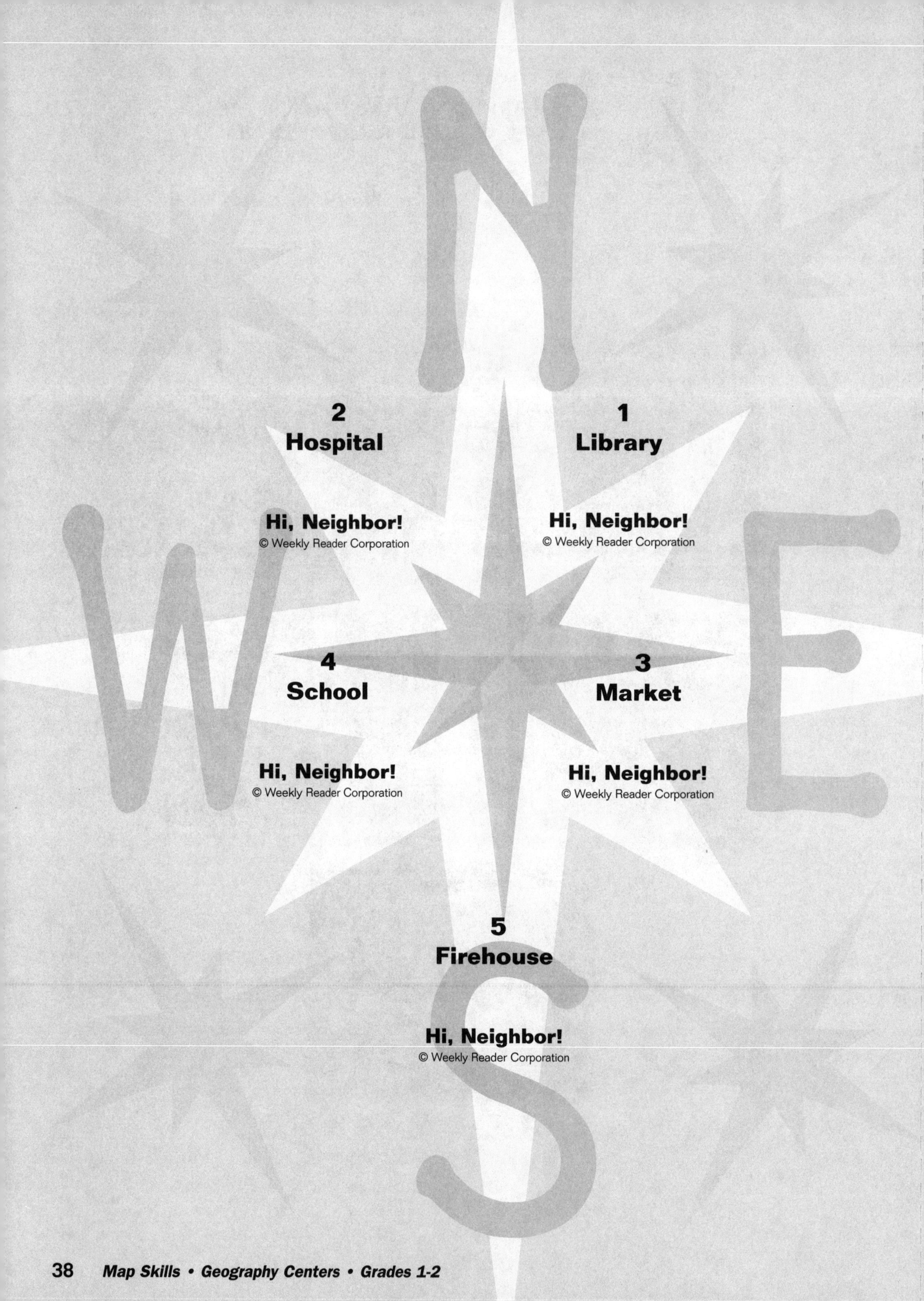

2
Hospital

Hi, Neighbor!
© Weekly Reader Corporation

1
Library

Hi, Neighbor!
© Weekly Reader Corporation

4
School

Hi, Neighbor!
© Weekly Reader Corporation

3
Market

Hi, Neighbor!
© Weekly Reader Corporation

5
Firehouse

Hi, Neighbor!
© Weekly Reader Corporation

Hi, Neighbor!

Hi, Neighbor!

Answers

Hi, Neighbor!

1. **hospital**

2. **firehouse**

3. **School Street**

4. **garden**

5. **Library Way**

6. **yellow**

Getting Directions

Learning About a Compass Rose

Get Ready!

- Prepare a folder following directions on page 3. Student instructions are on page 45, an activity mat is on page 47, activity cards are on page 49, and the answer key is on page 51.

- Make copies of the reproducible activity sheet on page 42 and put them in the left folder pocket.

- Laminate and cut apart the activity cards. Place the activity cards in an envelope or a self-locking bag. Put the activity mat and activity cards in the right folder pocket.

- Invite students to take the activity mat and cards from the folder.

- Tell students to look at the picture map and the little pictures below it. Ask them to place a direction card over the appropriate picture. Direction cards provide self-checking answers on the back.

- Have students complete the reproducible activity sheet. Students can check their answers by using the answer key.

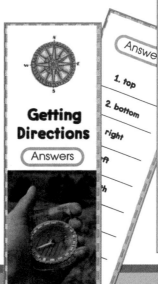

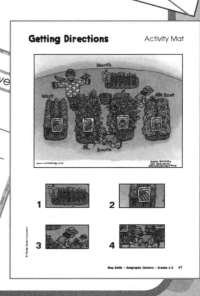

Getting Directions

Name_____

Read each sentence.
Choose a word from the word box.
Write it on the line.

1. On a compass rose, north is on the _____.
2. On a compass rose, south is on the _____.
3. On a compass rose, east is on the _____.
4. On a compass rose, west is on the _____.

> **bottom**　　　**left**　　　**top**　　　**right**

Read each sentence. Choose a word from the word box.
Write it on the line.

5. **N** on a compass rose stands for _____.
6. **S** on a compass rose stands for _____.
7. **E** on a compass rose stands for _____.
8. **W** on a compass rose stands for _____.

> **east**　　　**south**　　　**west**　　　**north**

WEEKLY WR READER

Getting Directions

Learning About a Compass Rose

WEEKLY WR READER

Getting Directions

Learning About a Compass Rose

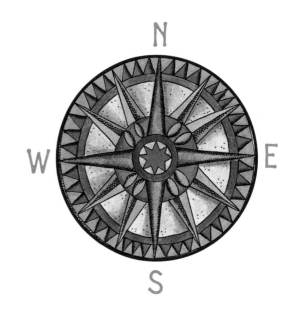

Where do the directions point?
Which way is east or west?
Use a compass rose,
It's easy. Do your best!

How to Use the Center

1. Take out the activity mat and direction word cards.

2. Look at each little picture on the bottom of the mat. Find where each one is located on the picture map. Is it north, south, east or west? Choose a direction word card and place it over the correct picture.

3. Complete the **Getting Directions** activity sheet.

4. Use the answer key to check your work.

Getting Directions

1

2

3

4

north

west

south

east

1

Getting Directions
© Weekly Reader Corporation

2

Getting Directions
© Weekly Reader Corporation

3

Getting Directions
© Weekly Reader Corporation

4

Getting Directions
© Weekly Reader Corporation

Getting Directions

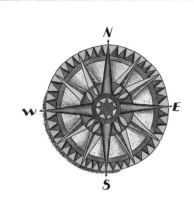

Getting Directions

Answers

Getting Directions

1. top

2. bottom

3. right

4. left

5. north

6. south

7. east

8. west

Which Way?

Using Direction Words

Get Ready!

- Prepare a folder following directions on page 3. Student instructions are on page 57, an activity mat is on page 59, activity cards are on page 61, and the answer key is on page 63.

- Make copies of the reproducible activity sheet on page 54 and put them in the left folder pocket.

- Laminate and cut apart the activity cards. Place the activity cards in an envelope or a self-locking bag. Put the activity mat and activity cards in the right folder pocket.

- Ask students to match each photo on the activity mat to a similar item on the picture map. Have students use the compass rose to determine in which direction the item is found on the map. Have students then place the correct direction word card on top of the photo on the mat. The activity cards provide self-checking answers on the back.

- Have students complete the reproducible activity sheet. Students can check their answers by using the answer key.

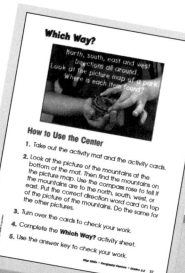

Which Way?

Name_____

Read each sentence. Look at the picture map. Circle the
correct direction word.

1. The cars are to the _____ of the school.

   east   west

2. The swings are to the _____ of the school.

   east   west

3. People are walking to the _____ of the school.

   north   south

4. A school bus is to the _____ of some people.

   north   south

5. The swings are to the _____ of the slide.

   north   south

Which Way?

Using Direction Words

WEEKLY W**R** **READER**

Which Way?

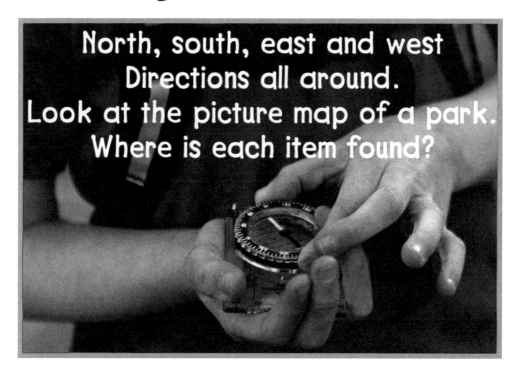

North, south, east and west
Directions all around.
Look at the picture map of a park.
Where is each item found?

How to Use the Center

1. Take out the activity mat and the activity cards.

2. Look at the picture of the mountains at the bottom of the mat. Then find the mountains on the picture map. Use the compass rose to tell if the mountains are to the north, south, west, or east. Put the correct direction word card on top of the picture of the mountains. Do the same for the other pictures.

3. Turn over the cards to check your work.

4. Complete the **Which Way?** activity sheet.

5. Use the answer key to check your work.

Which Way?

How do I find things in the park on this sunny day?

A compass rose with its directions helps me find the way!

1. mountains   2. park ranger   3. camera   4. hiker

Which Way?
Activity Cards

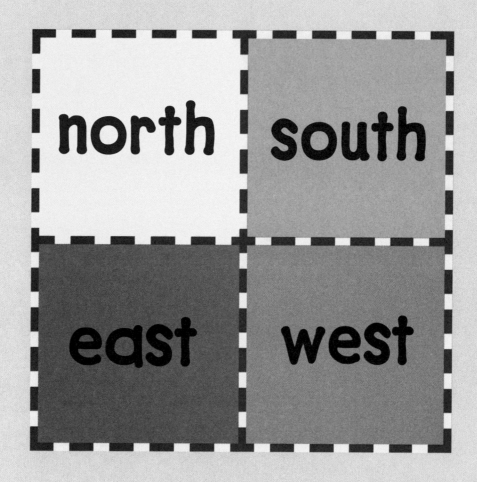

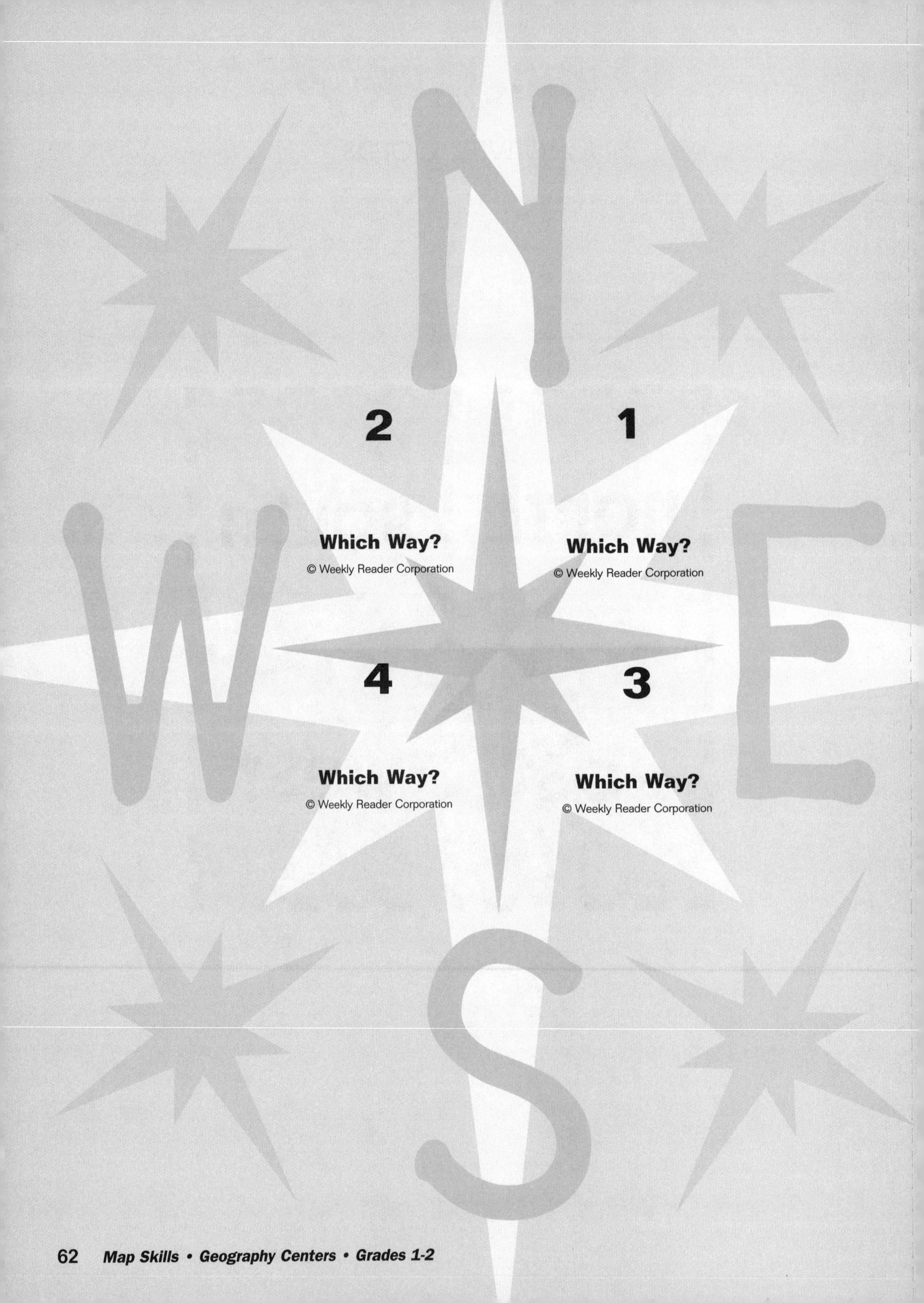

2

Which Way?

© Weekly Reader Corporation

1

Which Way?

© Weekly Reader Corporation

4

Which Way?

© Weekly Reader Corporation

3

Which Way?

© Weekly Reader Corporation

Which Way?

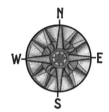

Which Way?

Answers

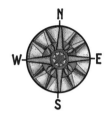

Which Way?

1. west

_____

2. east

_____

3. south

_____

4. north

_____

5. north

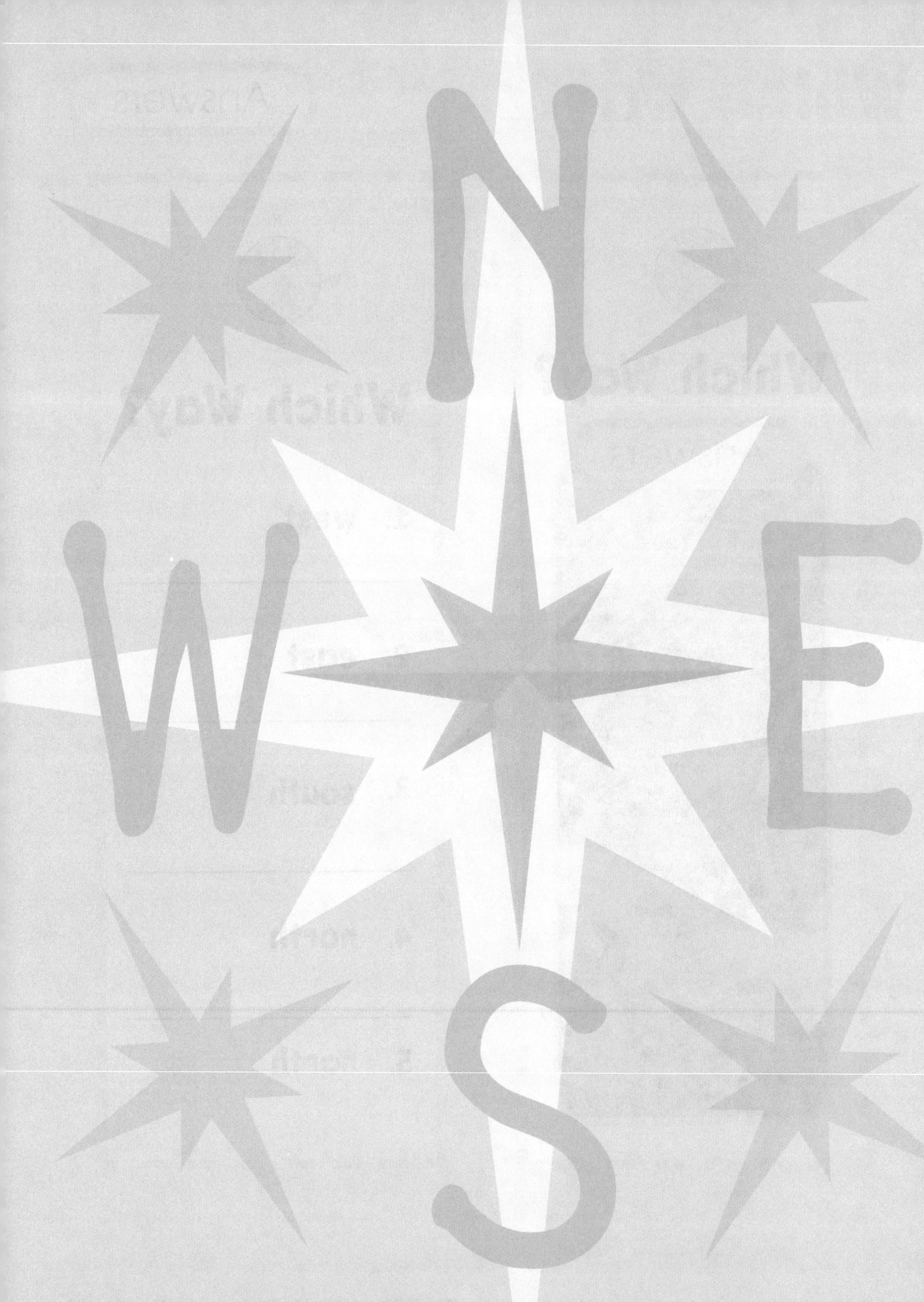
N
W
E
S

What Is a Map Key?

Understanding Map Keys and Map Symbols

Get Ready!

- Prepare a folder following directions on page 3. Student instructions are on page 69, an activity mat is on page 71, activity cards are on page 73, and the answer key is on page 75.

- Make copies of the reproducible activity sheet on page 66 and put them in the left folder pocket.

- Laminate and cut apart each set of activity cards. Put the land form cards and the Washington, D.C. cards in separate envelopes. Place the activity mat and both sets of cards in the right pocket folder.

- Invite students to take the activity mat and both sets of cards from the folder. First have students look at each photo at the top of the activity mat and find a card with a corresponding symbol to place on top of each photo. The back of the cards provide self-checking answers.

- Then ask students to look at the map of Washington, D.C. Have them match the word card with the correct building. The back of the cards provide self-checking answers.

- Have students complete the reproducible activity sheet. Students can check their answers by using the answer key.

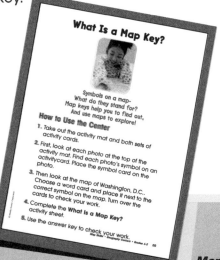

What Is A Map Key?

Name_____

The map has symbols that show the location of some things. Look at the Map Key and the map. Circle the correct word to complete the sentence.

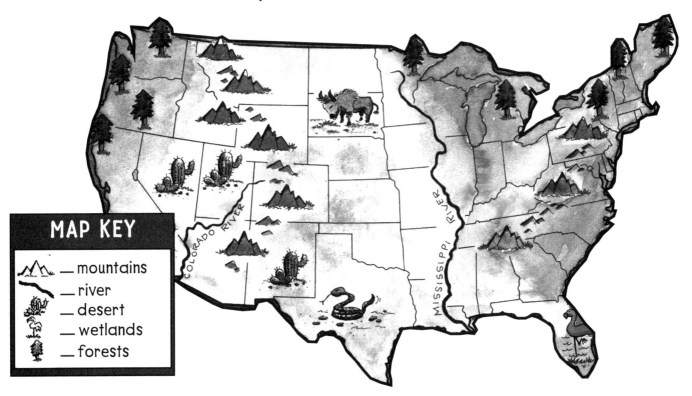

MAP KEY

- mountains
- river
- desert
- wetlands
- forests

1. The map shows _____ rivers. **two   three**

2. Deserts are on the _____ side of this map. **east   west**

3. The forests on this map are mostly to the _____. **north   south**

4. Wetlands on this map are to the_____. **north   south**

Write your answer on the line.
5. Trees on this map are symbols for _____.

What Is a Map Key?

Understanding Map Keys and Map Symbols

WEEKLY WR READER

What Is a Map Key?

Symbols on a map—What do they stand for?
Map keys help you to find out,
And use maps to explore!

How to Use the Center

1. Take out the activity mat and both sets of activity cards.

2. First, look at each photo at the top of the activity mat. Find each photo's symbol on an activity card. Place the symbol card on the photo.

3. Then look at the map of Washington, D.C. Choose a word card and place it next to the correct symbol on the map. Turn over the cards to check your work.

4. Complete the **What Is a Map Key?** activity sheet.

5. Use the answer key to check your work.

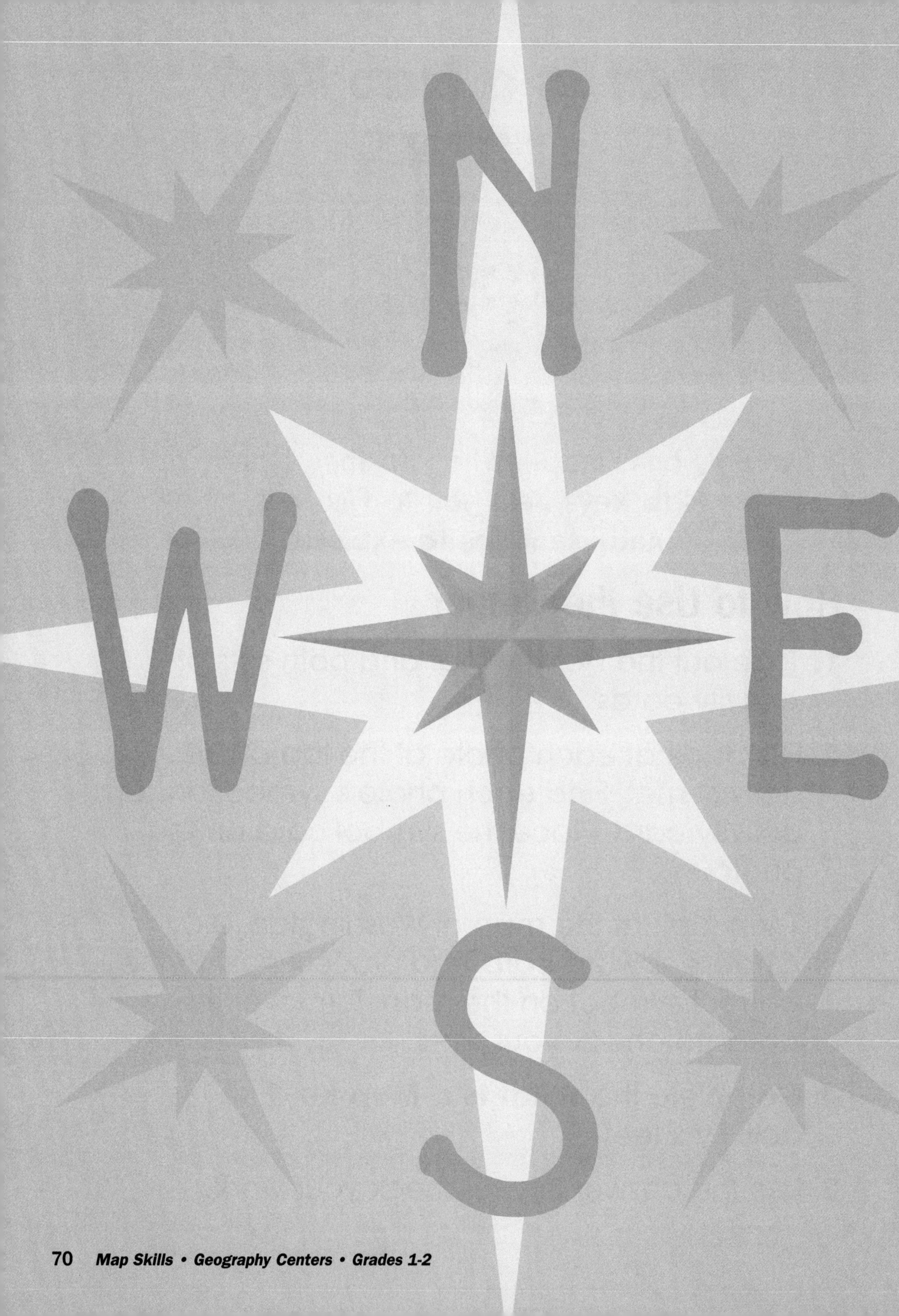
N
W
E
S

What Is a Map Key?

1. mountains **2. river** **3. road** **4. trees**

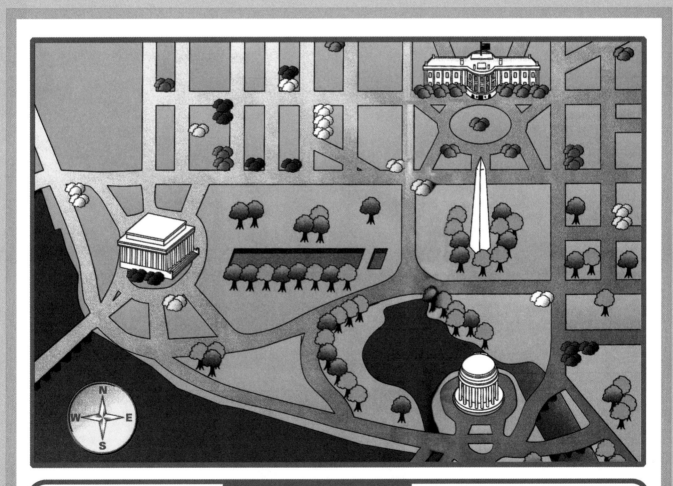

Map Key

White House **Jefferson Memorial** **Reflecting Pool** **Washington Monument** **Lincoln Memorial**

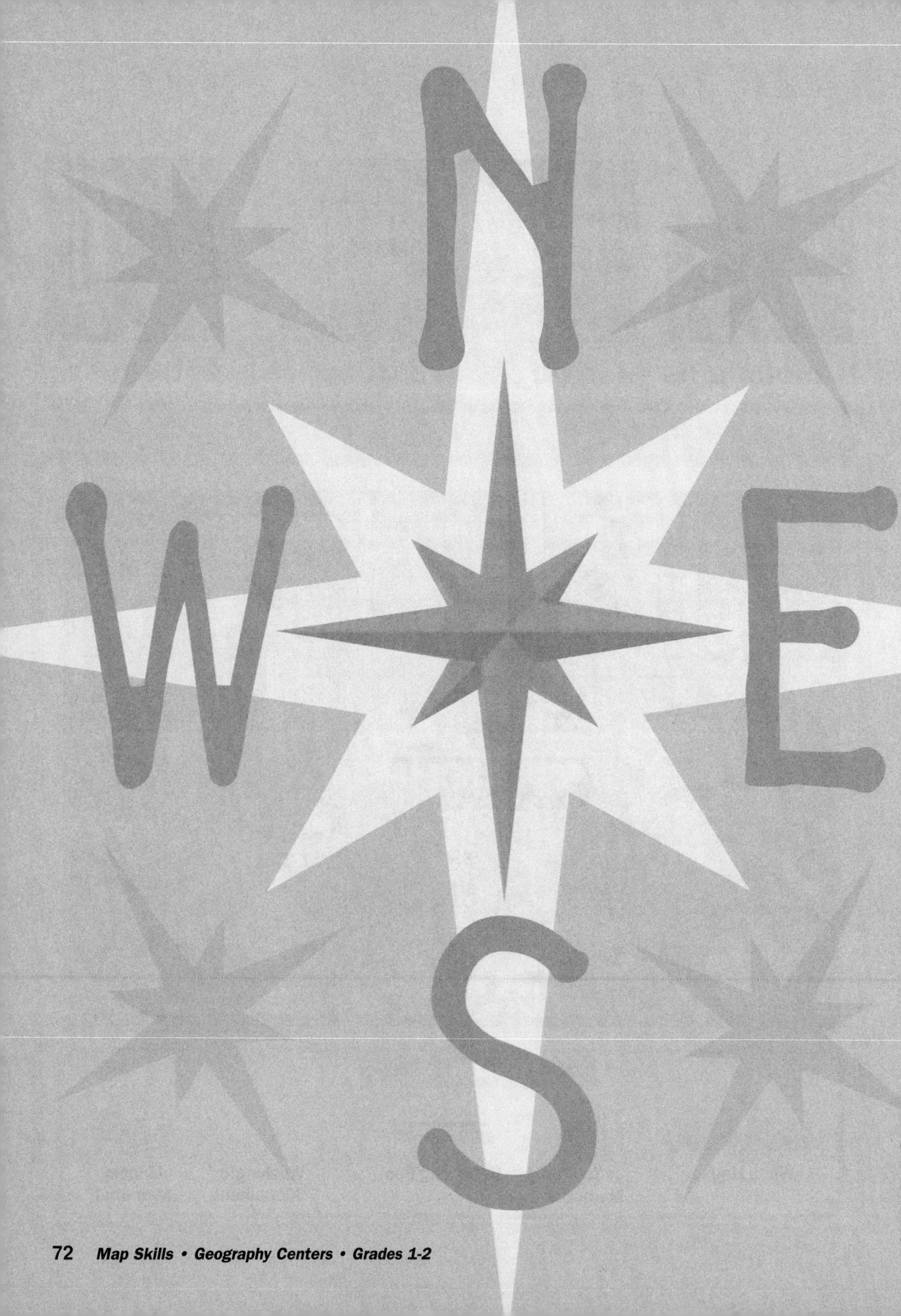
N
W
E
S

What Is a Map Key?
Activity Cards

White House	**Lincoln Memorial**
Washington Monument	**Jefferson Memorial**

2
river

What Is a Map Key?
© Weekly Reader Corporation

1
mountains

What Is a Map Key?
© Weekly Reader Corporation

3
road

What Is a Map Key?
© Weekly Reader Corporation

4
trees

What Is a Map Key?
© Weekly Reader Corporation

What Is a Map Key?
© Weekly Reader Corporation

What Is a Map Key?
© Weekly Reader Corporation

What Is a Map Key?
© Weekly Reader Corporation

What Is a Map Key?
© Weekly Reader Corporation

What Is a Map Key? Answers

What Is a Map Key?

Answers

What Is a Map Key?

1. two

_____

2. west

_____

3. north

_____

4. south

_____

5. forests

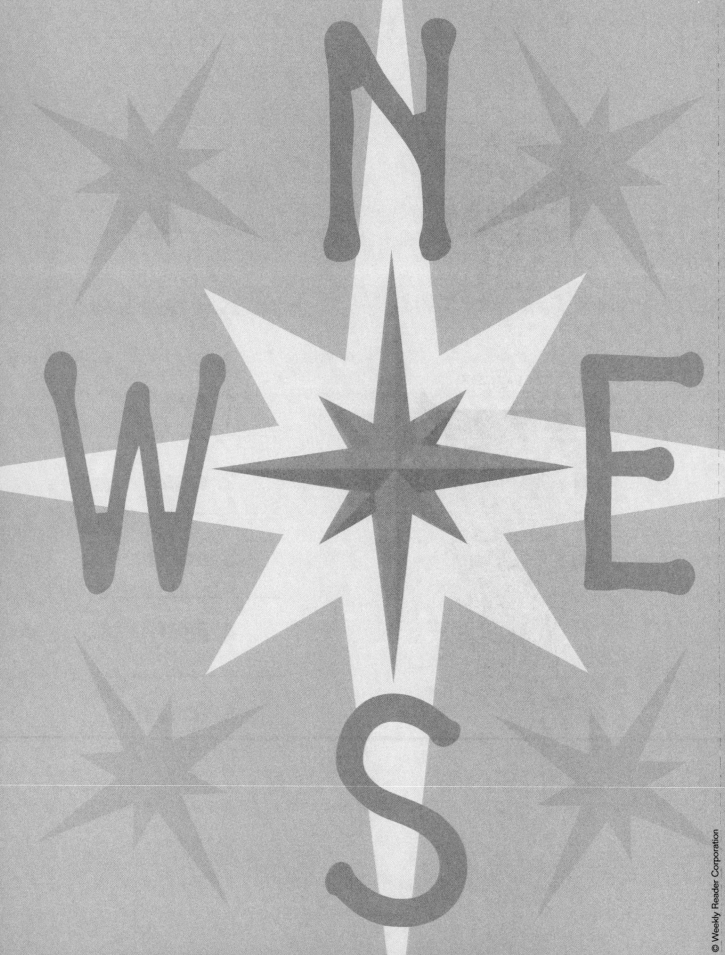

Land or Water?

Identifying Land and Water on a Map

Get Ready!

- Prepare a folder following directions on page 3. Student instructions are on page 81, an activity mat is on page 83, activity cards are on page 85, and the answer key is on page 87.

- Make copies of the reproducible activity sheet on page 78 and put them in the left folder pocket.

- Laminate and cut apart the activity cards. Place the activity cards in an envelope or a self-locking bag. Put the activity mat and activity cards in the right folder pocket.

- Invite students to take the activity mat and cards from the folder. Have them study the photos on the activity mat. Ask students to choose a card whose symbol and word match the photo. Have students place that card on top of the correct photo. The back of the cards provide self-checking answers.

- Have students complete the reproducible activity sheet. Students can check their answers by using the answer key.

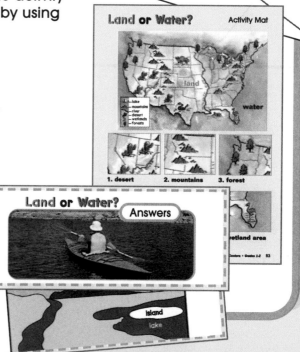

Land or Water?

Name_____

Read each sentence and follow the instructions.

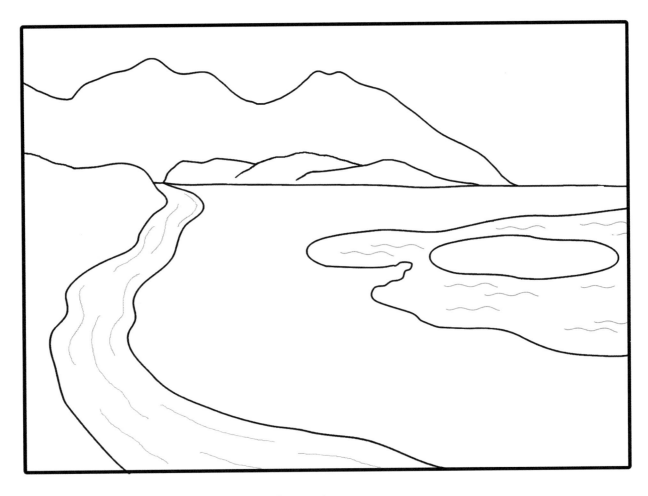

1. Find the mountains. Color them green.
2. Color the river blue.
3. Find the lake and write **lake** on it. Then color it blue.
4. Find the island in the lake. Write **island** on it.
5. Find the hills. Color them brown.
6. Flat land is called a plain. Color the plains light green.
7. Which is higher: **a mountain** or **a hill**?

Land or Water?

Identifying Land and Water on a Map

Photo Credit: Masterfile

WEEKLY **WR** READER

Land or Water?

Identifying Land and Water on a Map

Earth's land comes
in different shapes.
Do you know each
name?
Earth has oceans,
rivers, lakes,
Are those things all
the same?

How to Use the Center

1. Take out the activity mat and the activity cards.

2. Look at each map symbol on the mat. Find the card with a matching photograph. Place that card on top of the symbol. Turn over the cards to check your work.

3. Choose a photo card. Then find the place or places on the map that show the correct symbols for the photo.

4. Complete the **Land or Water?** activity sheet.

5. Use the answer key to check your work.

Land or Water?

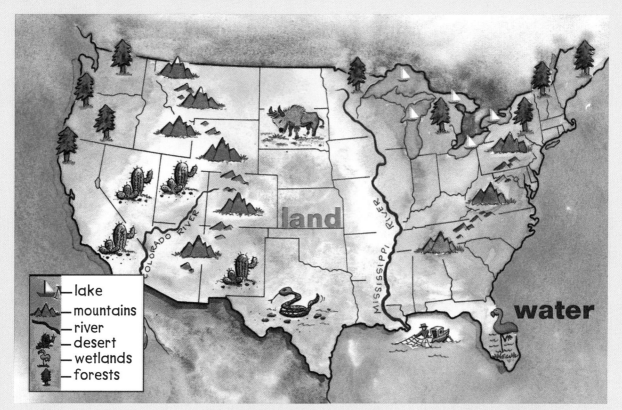

lake
mountains
river
desert
wetlands
forests

land

water

COLORADO RIVER

MISSISSIPPI RIVER

1. desert

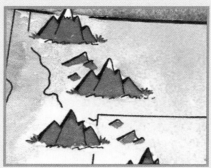

2. mountains

3. forest

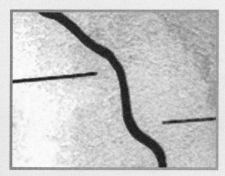

4. river

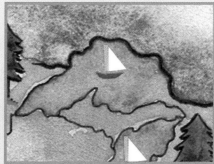

5. lake

6. wetland area

Land or Water?

Activity Cards

3

forest

Land or Water?
© Weekly Reader Corporation

1

desert

Land or Water?
© Weekly Reader Corporation

4

river

Land or Water?
© Weekly Reader Corporation

6

wetlands

Land or Water?
© Weekly Reader Corporation

5

lake

Land or Water?
© Weekly Reader Corporation

2

mountains

Land or Water?
© Weekly Reader Corporation

Land or Water?

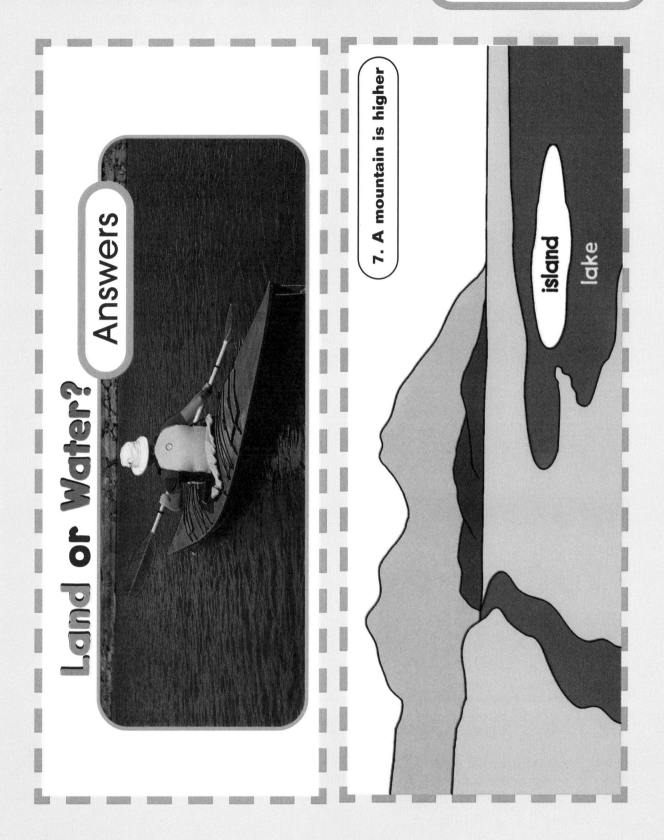

Answers

Land or Water?

7. A mountain is higher

island

lake

U.S. Neighbors

Understanding a U.S. Map In Relation to Canada and Mexico

Get Ready!

- Prepare a folder following directions on page 3. Student instructions are on page 93, an activity mat is on page 95, activity cards are on page 97, and the answer key is on page 99.

- Make copies of the reproducible activity sheet on page 90 and put them in the left folder pocket.

- Laminate and cut apart the activity cards and game pieces. Place them in an envelope or a self-locking bag. Put the activity mat and activity cards in the right folder pocket.

- Ask students to read a clue card and use it to find the correct place on the map. Have students place a red game piece on that place on the map. The back of the cards provide self-checking answers.

- Have students complete the reproducible activity sheet. Students can check their answers by using the answer key.

The United States is directly south of this country.

Washington, D.C. is the capital of this country.

U.S. Neighbors

Name_____

Choose a word or words from the word box
to complete each sentence.

1. Washington, D.C. is on the _____side of the
   United States.

2. Two countries, named_____and_____,
   touch the United States.

3. The_____Ocean touches the United States on
   the east.

4. If you were in the United States, which direction would
   you go to get to Mexico?_____

5. Alaska is part of the _____.

6. If you were in Mexico, what direction would
   you go to get to Canada?_____

---

south   United States   east

Canada   Atlantic   north   Mexico

U.S. Neighbors

Understanding a U.S. Map
In Relation to Canada and Mexico

WEEKLY WR READER

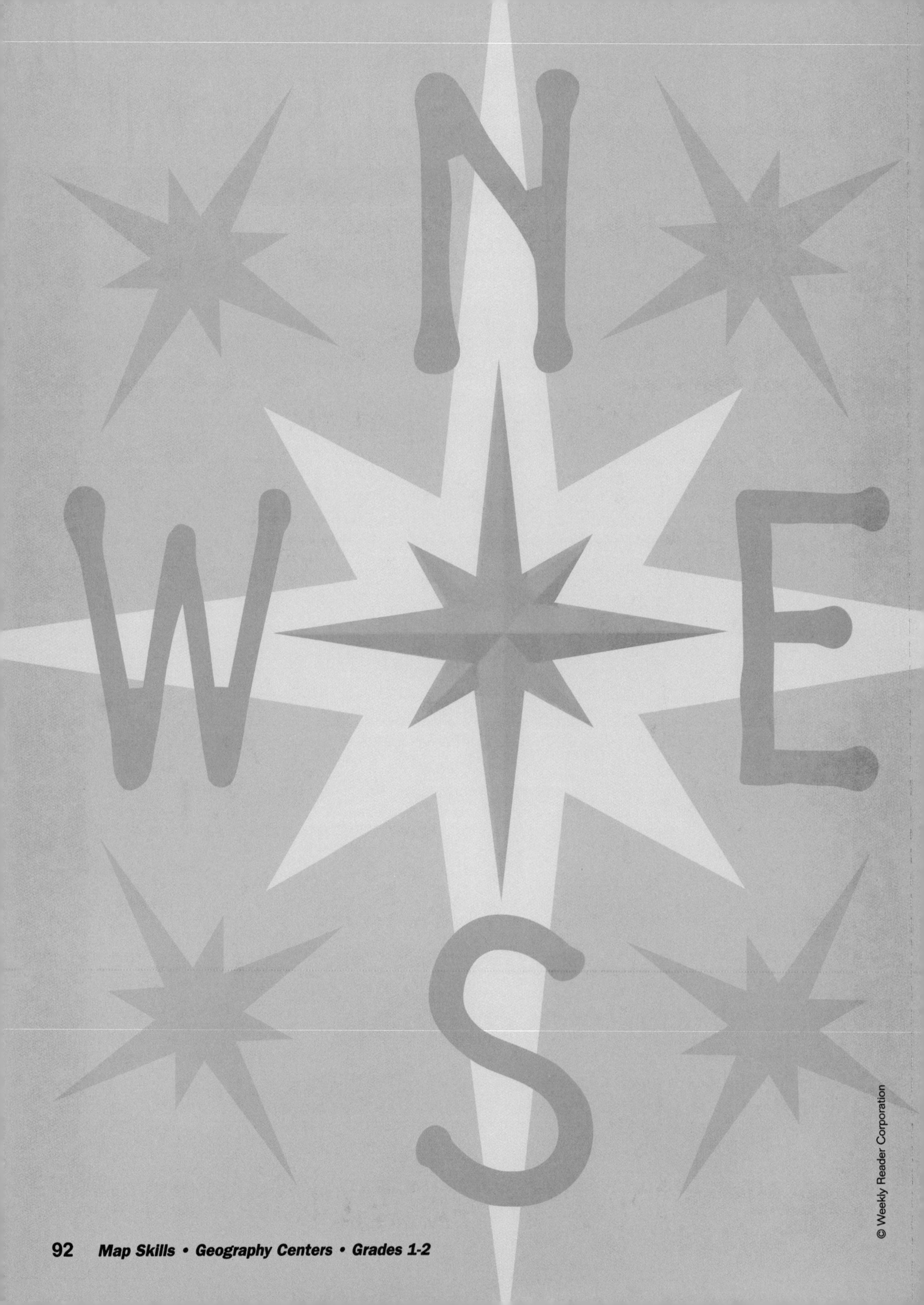
N
W
E
S

U.S. Neighbors

Our country has some neighbors
One above and one below.
What are those neighbors' names?
Canada and Mexico!

How to Use the Center

1. Take out the activity mat, activity cards, and round game pieces.

2. Read each activity card clue. Use the clue to find the correct place on the map. Put a red game piece on that place on the map.

3. Turn the cards over to check your work.

4. Complete the **U.S. Neighbors** activity sheet.

5. Use the answer key to check your work.

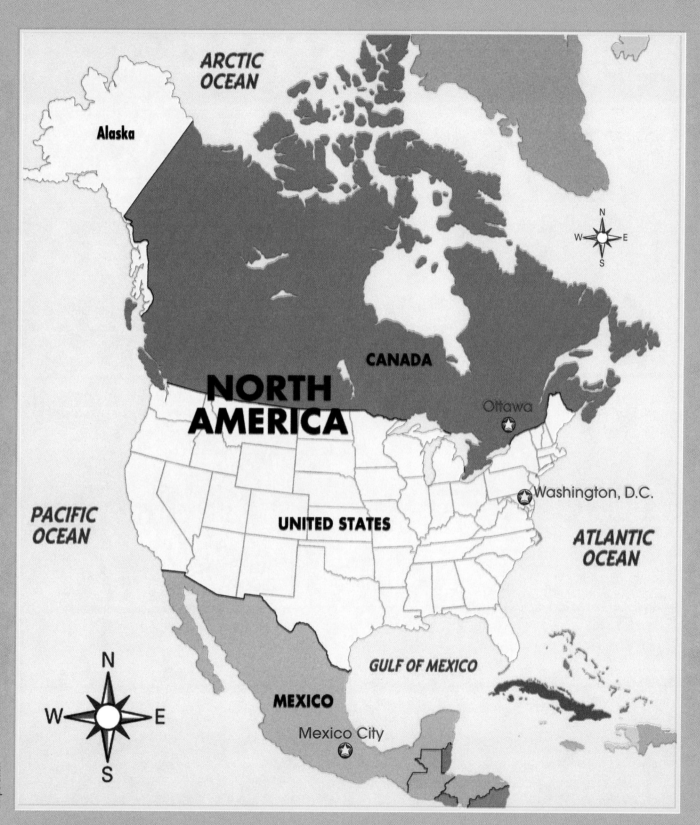

Activity Cards

1

The United States is directly south of this country.

2

Washington, D.C. is the capital of this country.

3

This country lies directly south of the United States.

4

This ocean touches the west side of United States.

5

This ocean touches the north side of Canada.

6

This body of water touches the east side of Mexico.

2

United States

U.S. Neighbors
© Weekly Reader Corporation

1

Canada

U.S. Neighbors
© Weekly Reader Corporation

4

Pacific Ocean

U.S. Neighbors
© Weekly Reader Corporation

3

Mexico

U.S. Neighbors
© Weekly Reader Corporation

6

Gulf of Mexico

U.S. Neighbors
© Weekly Reader Corporation

5

Arctic Ocean

U.S. Neighbors
© Weekly Reader Corporation

U.S. Neighbors

U.S. Neighbors

Answers

U.S. Neighbors

1. **east**

2. **Mexico and Canada**

3. **Atlantic**

4. **south**

5. **United States**

6. **north**

Carl Goes to California

Learning About a State Map
(Capital, Borders, Rivers)

Get Ready!

- Prepare a folder following directions on page 3. Student instructions are on page 105, an activity mat is on page 107, activity cards are on page 109, and the answer key is on page 111.

- Make copies of the reproducible activity sheet on page 102 and put them in the left folder pocket.

- Laminate and cut apart the activity cards. Place the activity cards in an envelope or a self-locking bag. Put the activity mat and activity cards in the right folder pocket.

- Ask students to read and use the clue cards to find the correct places on the California state map found on the mat. Have students write the name of the place on the correct line of the "Carl Goes to California" activity sheet. Students should then show Carl's path by drawing a line from place number one to place number two and so on.

- Students can check their answers by using the answer key.

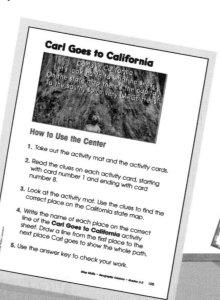

Carl Goes to California

Name_____

Read each card. Write the name of each place Carl visited on the lines below. Then draw a line to show Carl's path on the California map.

CALIFORNIA

Sacramento River

Sacramento ★ **Yosemite National Park**

Sacramento River

Monterey Bay Aquarium

Sequoia National Forest

Los Angeles ●

Mohave Desert

San Diego Zoo

1 _____

2 _____

3 _____

4 _____

5 _____

6 _____

7 _____

8 _____

WEEKLY WR READER

Carl Goes to California

Learning About a State Map
(Capital, Borders, Rivers)

WEEKLY WR READER

Carl Goes to California

Carl's in California.
Let's look north to what he sees.
On the state map there's the capital,
To the south, some very LARGE trees!

How to Use the Center

1. Take out the activity mat and the activity cards.

2. Read the clues on each activity card, starting with card number 1 and ending with card number 8.

3. Look at the activity mat. Use the clues to find the correct place on the California state map.

4. Then write the name of each place on the correct line of the **Carl Goes to California** activity sheet. Draw a line from the first place to the next place Carl goes to show the whole path.

5. Use the answer key to check your work.

Map Skills • Geography Centers • Grades 1-2

Carl Goes to California Activity Mat

CALIFORNIA

Sacramento River

Sacramento ☆ Yosemite National Park

Sacramento River

Monterey Bay Aquarium

Sequoia National Forest

Los Angeles ●

Mohave Desert

San Diego Zoo

MAP KEY

☆	capital
●	city
～	Sacramento River
-·-·-	state border
■	Yosemite National Park
🐟	Monterey Bay Aquarium
🐼	San Diego Zoo
🐢	Mohave Desert
🌲	Sequoia Forest

Carl Goes to California
Activity Cards

1. Carl is checking out a big river in the north.

2. Carl visits California's capital.

3. From there Carl goes south to a national park with rocky cliffs and waterfalls.

4. Next Carl goes west to see sea stars, sharks, and more!

5. Carl goes east to another national park to see really BIG trees.

6. Carl heads south to a dry place where tortoises and mule deer live.

7. Carl finally goes south to a city with a special zoo.

8. When Carl gets home he will say he had fun in _____!

2

Carl Goes to California
© Weekly Reader Corporation

1

Carl Goes to California
© Weekly Reader Corporation

4

Carl Goes to California
© Weekly Reader Corporation

3

Carl Goes to California
© Weekly Reader Corporation

6

Carl Goes to California
© Weekly Reader Corporation

5

Carl Goes to California
© Weekly Reader Corporation

8

Carl Goes to California
© Weekly Reader Corporation

7

Carl Goes to California
© Weekly Reader Corporation

Carl Goes to California

Answers

Carl Goes to California

1. Sacramento River

2. Sacramento

3. Yosemite National Park

4. Monterey Bay Aquarium

5. Sequoia National Forest

6. Mojave Desert

7. San Diego Zoo

8. California

What a Wonderful World

Get Ready!

- Prepare a folder following directions on page 3. Student instructions are on page 117, an activity mat is on pages 119 and 121, activity cards and game pieces are on page 123, and an activity sheet answer key is on page 125.

- Make copies of the reproducible activity sheet on page 114 and put them in the left folder pocket. Tape together the two pages of the activity mat and laminate it.

- Laminate and cut apart the activity cards. Place the activity cards in an envelope or a self-locking bag. Put the activity mat and activity cards in the right folder pocket.

- Ask students to read a card and decide if the answer should be "continent" or "ocean." Have students choose a "C" game piece for "continent" or an "O" game piece for "ocean" and put it on the correct place on the map on the activity mat. The back of the cards provide self-checking answers.

- Have students complete the reproducible activity sheet. Students can check their answers by using the answer key.

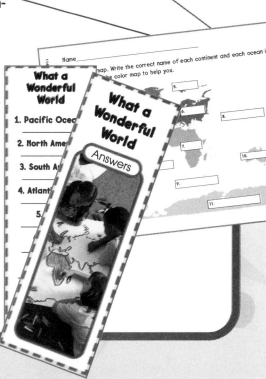

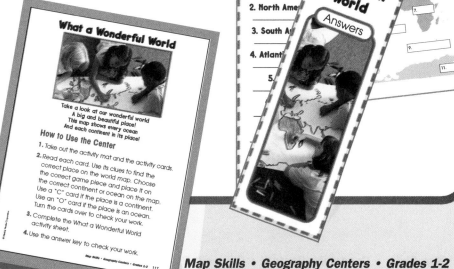

Name _____

Look at the map. Write the correct name of each continent and each ocean in the boxes. Use the color map to help you.

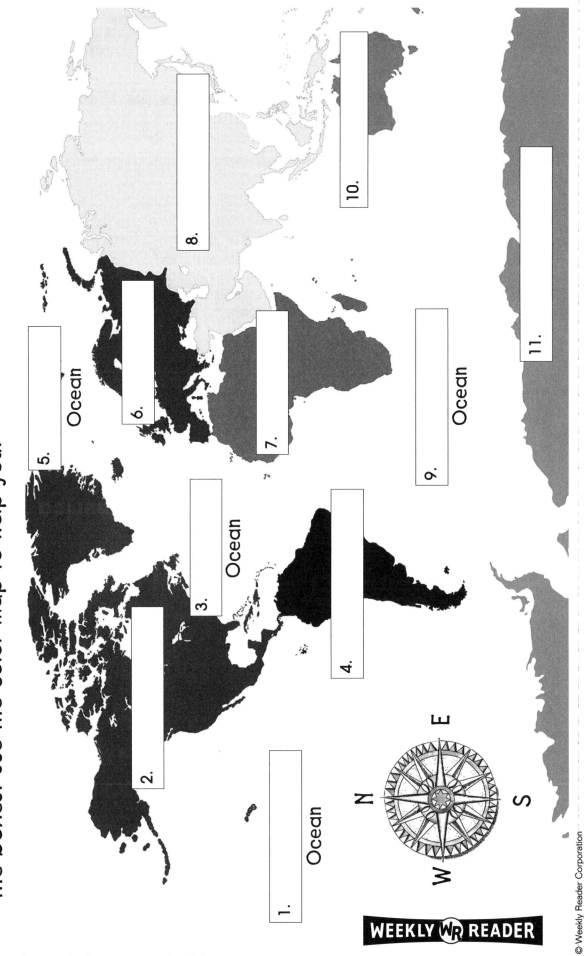

1. _____ Ocean

2. _____

3. _____ Ocean

4. _____

5. _____ Ocean

6. _____

7. _____

8. _____

9. _____ Ocean

10. _____

11. _____

WEEKLY WR READER

What a Wonderful World

Examining a World Map

WEEKLY WR READER

What a Wonderful World

Take a look at our wonderful world
A big and beautiful place!
The map shows every ocean
And each continent in its place!

How to Use the Center

1. Take out the activity mat and the activity cards.

2. Read each card. Use its clues to find the correct place on the world map. Choose the correct game piece and place it on the correct continent or ocean on the map. Use a "C" card if the place is a continent. Use an "O" card if the place is an ocean. Turn the cards over to check your work.

3. Complete the What a Wonderful World activity sheet.

4. Use the answer key to check your work.

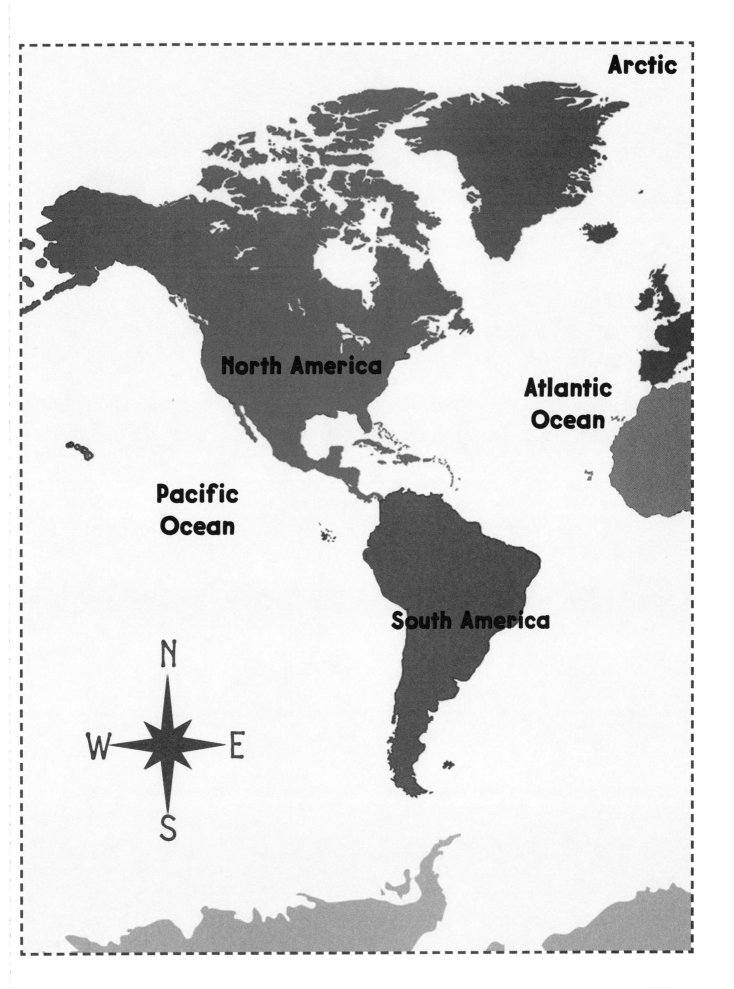

Arctic

North America

Atlantic
Ocean

Pacific
Ocean

South America

N

W E

S

N

W   E

S

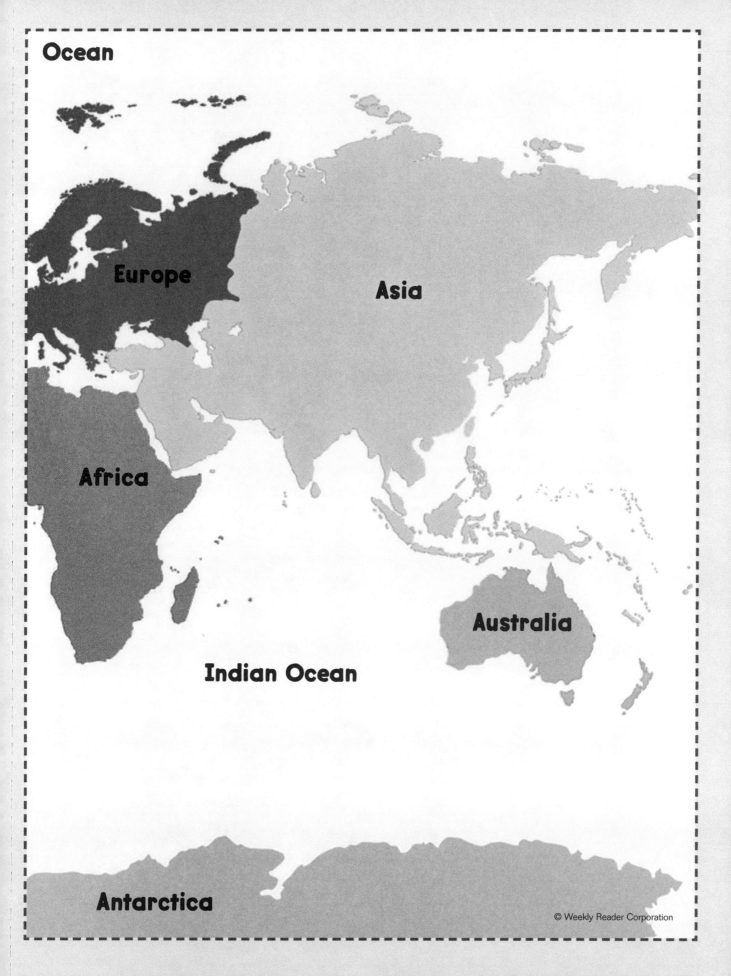

Ocean

Europe

Asia

Africa

Australia

Indian Ocean

Antarctica

© Weekly Reader Corporation

N

W E

S

1. I am above and west of South America.
I am_____.

2. I am right above Europe and Asia.
I am_____.

3. I am below and east of North America.
I am _____.

4. I am between Australia and the bottom part of Africa. I am _____.

5. On the map, I am south of all the oceans.
I am _____.

6. I touch the east side of Europe and Africa .
I am _____.

7. I touch North and South America on the west. I am _____.

8. I touch North and South America on the east. I am _____.

2

an ocean:
Arctic Ocean

What a Wonderful World

© Weekly Reader Corporation

1

a continent:
North America

What a Wonderful World

© Weekly Reader Corporation

4

an ocean:
Indian Ocean

What a Wonderful World

© Weekly Reader Corporation

3

a continent:
South America

What a Wonderful World

© Weekly Reader Corporation

6

a continent:
Asia

What a Wonderful World

© Weekly Reader Corporation

5

a continent:
Antarctica

What a Wonderful World

© Weekly Reader Corporation

8

an ocean:
Atlantic Ocean

What a Wonderful World

© Weekly Reader Corporation

7

an ocean:
Pacific Ocean

What a Wonderful World

© Weekly Reader Corporation

What a Wonderful World

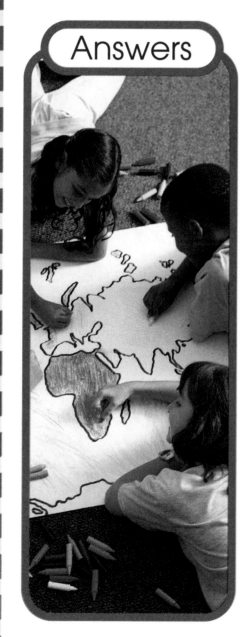

What a Wonderful World

Answers

What a Wonderful World

1. Pacific Ocean

2. North America

3. Atlantic Ocean

4. South America

5. Arctic Ocean

6. Europe

7. Africa

8. Asia

9. Indian Ocean

10. Australia

11. Antarctica

Name_____

Let's Review #1

Do You Know Map Skills?

Read each sentence. Circle Yes or No

1. A map is a drawing of a place.   Yes   No

2. A river is filled with water.   Yes   No

3. Maps can show neighborhoods, states,

   and countries.   Yes   No

4. A compass rose is a kind of flower.   Yes   No

5. A mountain is land that is very high.   Yes   No

6. North, south, east, and west are directions

   on a map.   Yes   No

- ✂

Let's Review Answer Key

Let's Review #1:

1. yes, 2. yes, 3. yes, 4. no, 5. yes, 6. yes

Let's Review #1:

1. Washington, 2. Colorado, 3. New Mexico,

4. Pacific Ocean, 5. Montana, 6. Texas, 7. Nevada,

8. Answers will vary.

Name_____

Let's Review #2

Look at the map. Write your answer on the line.

Note: Alaska and Hawaii are not in position and are not drawn to scale.

1. Which state touches Oregon on the north side? _____

2. Which state touches Kansas on the west side?_____

3. Which state touches Arizona on the east side? _____

4. Which ocean touches California on the west side? _____

5. Which State is farther north, Wyoming or Montana? _____

6. Which state is farther south, Kansas or Texas? _____

7. Which state touches Utah on the west side? _____

8. Find and circle your state.